LONG CIRCULAR WALKS IN CHESHIRE

by

JOHN N. MERRILL

Maps and photographs by John N. Merrill

TRAIL CREST PUBLICATIONS Ltd.,
- *"from footprint to finished book."*

1993

Sandia Mountains
New Mexico. USA

TRAIL CRES
PUBLICATION$
Ltd.
WINSTER
MATLOCK
DERBYSHIRE
DE4 2D(
 (0629) 82635◄
(0629) 82635◄

Concieved, edited, typeset, designed, paged, printed, marketed and distributed by John N. Merrill.

© Text & walks - John N. Merrill 1993
© Maps & photographs - John N. Merrill 1993.

First Published - April 1993.

ISBN 0 874754 14 4

U.S.A.
office -
P.O.Box 124.
Santa Rosa,
New Mexico.
88435
U.S.A.

Please note - The maps in this guide are purely illustrative. You are encouraged to use the appropriate 1:25,000 O.S. map.

Meticulous research has been undertaken to ensure that this publication is highly accurate at the time of going to press. The publishers, however, cannot be held responsible for alterations, errors or omissions, but they would welcome notification of such for future editions.

Typeset in - Bookman bold, italic and plain 9pt and 18pt.

Printed by - John N. Merrill at Milne House, Speedwell Mill, Miller's Green, Wirksworth, Derbyshire. DE4 4BL

Cover sketch by John Creber "Jenkin Chapel, Saltersford."
- © Trail Crest Publications Ltd. 1993.

An all British product.

The author on the summit of Mt.Taylor (11,301ft.), New Mexico.

ABOUT JOHN N. MERRILL

Born in the flatlands of Bedfordshire he soon moved to Sheffield and discovered the joy of the countryside in the Peak District, where he lives. A keen walker who travels the world exploring mountains and trails. Over the last twenty years he has walked more than 150,000 miles and worn out over sixty pairs of boots. He has written more than 120 walk guides to areas in Britain and abroad, and created numerous challenge walks which have been used to raise more than £500,000 for charity. New Mexico, USA is his second home.

CONTENTS

INTRODUCTION

At first glance you might think Cheshire is level walking but in reality it has some impressive hills which are a delight to walk in. I completed this collection of walks over a year, slowly piecing together different ideas. My aim has been simple - to illustrate in twelve walks of ten to sixteen miles long the variety of walking found in the county. Some are relatively flat following some of the canals that meander through the county while others are more hilly exploring the Peakland hills of Cheshire and the hills of the Sandstone country.

On the east side is the Gritstone Trail, the Ridge of Kerridge, and the magnificent hill - Shutlingsloe. In the middle is Prestbury and the gritstone country around Alderley Edge. Southwards is the attractive Peover area, Vale Royal, Nantwich and the Shropshire Union Canal and its branches. In the deep south is Grindley Brook and the matchless village of Marbury. Whilst westwards is Helsby crag, the Peckforton Hills and Delamere Forest. Combined they are outstanding walking areas.

Here then is a collection of some of my favourite day walks in Cheshire - some hard, some easy - and most with an inn en route. I have derived many hours of pleasure exploring areas I only knew briefly and areas more familiar but approached from different routes. I hope you will follow in my footsteps and become like me, impressed at the variety of walking in Cheshire.

Happy walking!
John N. Merrill. 1993.

Bow Stones - Lyme Park walk.

Llangollen Canal - Marbury walk.

Whilst every care is taken detailing and describing the walk in this book, it should be borne in mind that the countryside changes by the seasons and the work of man. I have described the walk to the best of my ability, detailing what I have found on the walk in the way of stiles and signs. Obviously with the passage of time stiles become broken or replaced by a ladder stile or even a small gate. Signs too have a habit of being broken or pushed over. All the route follow rights of way and only on rare occasions will you have to overcome obstacles in its path, such as a barbed wire fence or electric fence. On rare occasions rights of way are rerouted and these ammendments are included in the next edition.

The seasons bring occasional problems whilst out walking which should also be borne in mind. In the height of summer paths become overgrown and you will have to fight your way through in a few places. In low lying areas the fields are often full of crops, and although the pathline goes straight across it may be more practical to walk round the field edge to get to the next stile or gate. In summer the ground is generally dry but in autumn and winter, especially because of our climate, the surface can be decidedly wet and slippery; sometimes even gluttonous mud!

These comments are part of countryside walking which help to make your walk more interesting or briefly frustrating. Standing in a farmyard up to your ankles in mud might not be funny at the time but upon reflection was one of the highlights of the walk!

The mileage for each walk is based on three calculations -

1. pedometer reading.
2. the route map measured on the map.
3. the time I took for the walk.

I believe the figure stated for each walk to be very accurate but we all walk differently and not always in a straight line! The time allowed for each walk is on the generous side and does not include pub stops etc. The figure is based on the fact that on average a person walks 2 1/2 miles an hours but less in hilly terrain.

LAMALOAD RESERVOIR & LYME PARK - 15 MILES

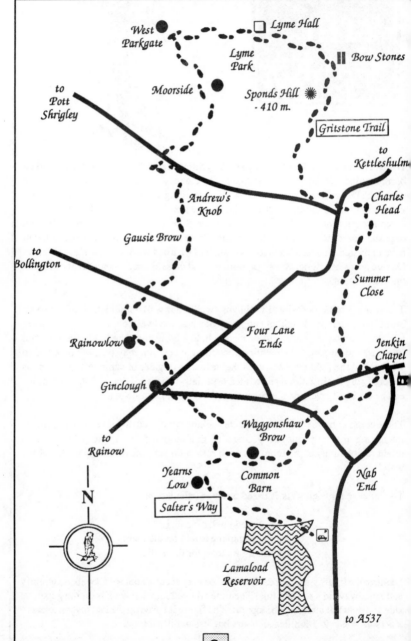

LAMALOAD RESERVOIR & LYME PARK
- 15 MILES
- allow 5 to 6 hours.

- Lamaload Reservoir Car Park - Salter's Way - Jenkin Chapel - Summer Close - Charles Head Farm - Gritstone Trail - Sponds Hill - Bow Stones - Lyme Park - Lyme Hall - Knott Gate - West Parkgate - Bakestonedale Moor - Gausie Brow - Billinge Head Farm - Back-of-the-Crofts - Ginclough - Yearns Low - Lamaload Reservoir.

O.S. MAP *- 1:25,000 Pathfinder Series Sheet Nos. SJ 87/97 - Macclesfield & Alderley Edge and Sheet No. 741 (SJ 88/98) - Stockport (South).*

P *- Lamaload Reservoir. Grid Ref. 975754.*

- None on the walk - sorry! Tearoom at Lyme Park.

ABOUT THE WALK - I did this walk as my 1993 New Years Day "wake up"! This probably accounts why there is no inn on this walk, as I set off every New Years Day with a bottle of wine, half a turkey and a massive slice of Christmas cake! I only return when I have run out of food and drink. However, the walk itself is magnificent and if you have a crystal clear day, like I had, you are in for a great walk. First you head northwards doing a section of the Salter's Way before gaining the Gritstone Trail and Lyme Park. The views on this section to Kinder are impressive. You return following little used paths over rugged terrain - the final hills before the Cheshire Plain - before retracing your starting out path back to Lamaload Reservoir. The walk is done anti-clockwise.

WALKING INSTRUCTIONS - From the car park at Lamaload Reservoir walk towards the reservoir passing the toilet block on your left to reach a stile. Continue along the northern edge of the reservoir on a track to a stile and footpath sign. Here you descend aiming for the righthand side of the waterboard works. Approaching the first house turn right at a stile and join the Salter's Way. You soon bear left and gradually ascend on a track to Yearns Low. Just after the buildings the track bears left and you keep right with the wall on your right to a stile. Here turn right with a wall on your left and walk through Common Barn Farm. Beyond the farm keep the wall on your left to a stile. Then cross an open field to another stile and gain a track along Waggonshaw Brow. Less than 1/2 mile from the farm reach a road. Turn left and in 50 yards right at a stile and footpath sign. Follow the path to more stiles and a small pine plantation. Descend through it to a gate and onto another stile. Then keep the hedge on your left to a footbridge and stile. The Salter's Way now turns right to Saltersford Hall where it ends close to the Cheshire/Derbyshire boundary. You keep straight ahead to the solitary Jenkin Chapel.

Turn left along the road for 100 yards to a stile and footpath sign on your right. Soon gain a track and pass Crabtree Farm and continue onto a wooded area where the track bears left to another farm and bridge over a stream. Continue to Summer Close and just beyond the farm ascend to a gate on your left and turn right. The path is defined and well stiled as it contours round the slope to Charles Head Farm 1/2 mile away. Follow the lefthand track at the farm and ascend to the road at Charles Head little over 1/4 mile away. Turn right then left and follow a lane for 1/4 mile to a stile and the Gritstone Trail on your right. Turn right and follow the track for 1/2 mile to Sponds Hill - 410m. Just before it is a viewfinder tablet, showing the location of the major places in the area, and placed here by the C.P.R.E. Continue on the trail to Bow Stones, little over 1/2 mile away.

Turn left just before the stones, still on the Gritstone Trail and now entering Lyme Park. Descend the moorland on a wide track to a ladder stile and pine plantation. Continue through the trees for less than 1/4 mile and turn right, leaving the trail, heading directly for Lyme Hall. Overlooking the hall and lake turn left to the main car park. Pass the northern end on the Gritstone Trail and follow the tarmaced road keeping to the lefthand one in a short distance to reach Knott Gate. Go through the gate and walk along the drive through woodland and rhoderdendrons - Hase Bank Wood - to West Parkgate. Gaining the road turn left to Shrigley Road. Here turn left by the Methodist Chapel and follow the track past Green Close Farm. This soon becomes a path as you ascend with the perimeter wall of Lyme Park on your left. In 1/2 mile approach Moorside and bear right to a stile. Here turn right on a track for a few yards to the righthand side of Keepers Cottage. Here turn left, signed Bowstones, plaque No. 154. Keep the wall on your left as you ascend and in more than 1/4 mile you loose it and reach a stile. Turn right on a track and start descending over Bakestonedale Moor to a minor road 1/2 mile away.

Turn left then right at a stile and footpath sign and keep a wall on your right. At the end of the field turn left and keep the wall still on your right to a stile. Turn right with a wall on your left descend to another stile. Here you descend steeply down Gausie Brow and onto a footbridge over Black Brook. Cross Mellow Brook and turn left at a stile and ascend, soon having a fence on your left and gain a stile. Continue on to another and gain a track which you follow to the road near Billinge Head Farm. Turn left then right and follow a track with a pine plantation on your right. In 1/4 mile turn left and follow the track past some of the houses of Rainowlow to Back-of-the-Crofts. Here turn left at the stile and walk beside the wall on your right to a stile and onto another at the road at Ginclough. Turn right and in a few yards past the house on your left is a footpath sign, and turn left. The pathline keeps near the wall on your left to two stiles before bearing right on a track which becomes stone flagged. Continue on guided by the stiles and in 1/4 mile you are back in familiar territory. Gain a stile and to your left is Common Barn you walked through four hours ago! Keep the wall on your left and descend to Yearns Low and down the track to the water works. Here turn left and ascend back to Lamaload Reservoir and retrace your steps back to the car park.

Lyme Hall.

PRESTBURY & ALDERLEY EDGE - 13 MILES

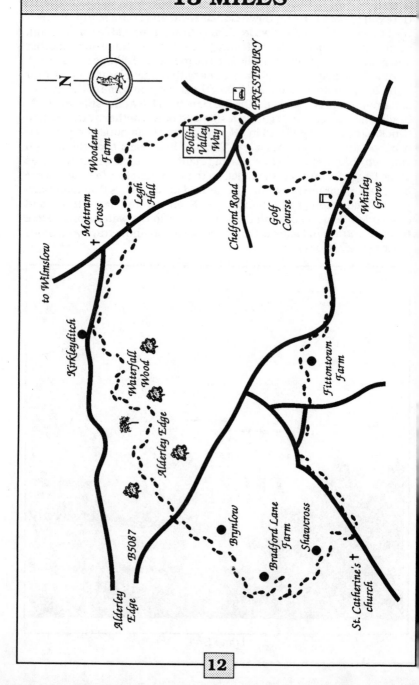

PRESTBURY & ALDERLEY EDGE
- 13 MILES
- allow 4 1/2 hours.

- Prestbury - Bollin Valley Way - Spittle House - Woodend Farm - Legh Hall - Mottram - Kirkleyditch - Clock House Wood - Alderley Edge - The Topps Farm - Bradford Lane Farm - Hocker Lane - Shawcross - Birtles Church - Highlees - Whirley Farm - Fittontown Farm - Whirley Grove - Fallibroome Farm - Prestbury Golf Course - Prestbury.

O.S. MAP *1:25,000 Pathfinder Series Sheet No. SJ 87/97 - Macclesfield & Alderley Edge.*

- Prestbury - off Shirleys Drive. Grid Ref. SK902768.

- None on the route! Several in Prestbury. One just off the route in Mottram. Wizard Tearoom just off the route at Alderley Edge.

ABOUT THE WALK - Prestbury is a particularly attractive village and well worth exploring. The walk takes you into beautiful countryside, to the wooded slopes of Alderley Edge; en route passing several impressive halls. You traverse old lanes to an octagonal church tower, before road and path walking back to Prestbury via its golf course. As you walk westwards you have views to Jodrell Bank Telescope and as you return views to the Peakland hills.

WALKING INSTRUCTIONS - From the car park just off Shirley's Drive, follow the signed path to the village and turn right, passing the stocks and church dedicated to St. Peter. Opposite is the impressive National Westminster Bank - the old priests house dated about 1580. Cross the River Bollin and immediately turn left along Bollin Grove. Continue straight ahead past a Methodist church on your right and at the end of the road gain a track, signed Bollin Valley Way. Pass a football field on your left and keep on the track for less than 1/4 mile to a footpath junction. Turn left and cross the river, following the signed path - "Mottram". Gain a stile and bear right and walk around the lefthand side of Spittle House before gaining some steps and a footbridge. Afterwards keep to the lefthand side of the field to a stile and track. Follow this past Woodend Farm to a stile. Bear right and follow

13

the faint path along the lefthand side of the field and ascend gently to the field corner with a horses graveyard. Bear right to a kissing gate then left along the road with Legh Hall to your right. Just past the end of the lake turn right at a stile and cross the righthand side of the field to a stile, path sign and minor road on the outskirts of Mottram - there is an inn along this road to your right!

Cross the road to your left to a track and path sign - Priest Lane. The track soon bears right and descends towards a thatched cottage. Just before it turn right and follow the signed path for Priest lane, descending to a footbridge then on to Brook House Farm. Cross the road and keep ahead on a track to gain Priest Lane. Turn left and ascend gently to Kirkleyditch, just over 1/4 mile away. Turn left, as footpath signed, by house No. 2. Keep to the righthand side of the field to reach a footbridge over Pott Brook. In another 200 yards cross another before ascending and joining a track towards the woodland of Alderley Edge. Where the track turns left keep straight ahead over a stile and onto a sunken path. Where this turns left, in a few yards, leave it and ascend steeply to the summit and track close to a National Trust sign on your right. Turn right on the track descending through the woodland. Where the path divides keep to the lefthand path and ascend soon keeping to the lefthand side of the wood - Waterfall Wood. Follow the path round to your left and up a ravine to the waterfall. Cross over and walk down the otherside, soon swinging left into Dickens Wood. Where the path divides take the righthand one and gain the main Alderley Edge path. Turn right along this track to the summit of the rocks and its view to Manchester Airport. Follow the path round to your left but take the lower path which leads towards the Beacon and a wall. Continue beside it and on the lefthand edge of the wood to a path junction - to your right and down in the trees is the Wizard's Well. Turn left along the track to the B5087 road, parking area and sign - "To the Edge."

Cross the road to a stile by a wooden gate. Keep to the edge of the field and in less than 1/4 mile reach a pond and turn left along a track. Keep straight ahead at all the junctions and in 200 yards reach a crossroads of tracks. Go straight across and in 1/4 mile pass a small rocky outcrop on your left before gaining the minor road near Brynlow. Turn right and soon pass the Topps Farm. A few yards later opposite the next farm - The Butts - turn left over a stile and follow the path along the edge of the fields to the lane near Bradford Lane Farm. Turn right along the cobbled lane to its junction with Hocker Lane. Turn left along Hocker Lane and keep on the lane for the next mile, passing Hayman's Farm and Acton Farm on your left. At the road junction just beyond - Shawcross - turn right - signed to Jarmans Farm. Keep on this track for 1/2 mile to Church Cottage and the minor road near Birtles church dedicated to St. Catherine, on your right - worth a visit to see the unusual octagonal tower.

Turn left along the road for 1/4 mile to a track and footpath sign on your right. Turn right along the track and walk through Long Highlees Wood. On the otherside turn left, as footpath signed and walk around the field edge on your left to a track from Highlees. Ascend to the top of the track and turn right and walk along the field edge to a gate in the far corner. Descend the track beyond in Highlees Wood. Follow the track round to your left and bear right at the stile and cross the field to a stile opposite Whirley Farm. Turn left up the road for a 1/3 mile to a crossroads. Turn right along a track to Fittontown Farm. Where the track turns left into the farm, keep straight ahead to a gate and descend the hedged track which soon comes into woodland before gaining the B5087 road. Turn right and follow the road for 1/2 mile - there is a path most of the way on the righthand side. Pass the Prestbury boundary sign and 1/4 mile later turn left at the footpath sign by Fallibroome Farm. Just past the farm turn right at a stile and cross the field to another stile and a rugby field. Walk around the lefthand edge of the field and keep straight ahead across a road and past houses on your right to the golf club road. Cross over and follow the yellow posts across the course and around to your left to a kissing gate and Chelford Road. Turn right and descend the road back into Prestbury.

Old Priest's House - 1580 - Prestbury.

PLUMLEY & LOWER PEOVER - 11 MILES

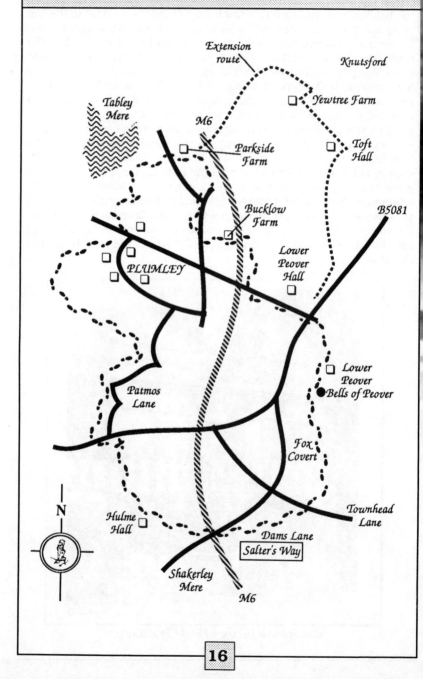

PLUMLEY
& LOWER PEOVER
- 11 MILES
- allow 4 hours.

■■ ■■ ■■ - *Plumley - Whitehouse Farm - Royd Wood - Parkside Cottage - Parkside Farm - Diamond Farm - Bucklow Farm - Plumley Moor Road - Lower Peover - Fox Covert - Old Mill Farm - Dam's Lane - Hulme Hall - Patmos Lane - Brookhouse Farm - Plumley.*

4 mile extension to route - Parkside Farm - Blackhill Farm - Whitehouse Farm - Bexton Hall - Toft Hall - Plumleylane Farm - Lower Peover.

O.S. MAP *1:25,000 Pathfinder Series No. 758 (SJ 67/77) - Northwich & Knutsford.*

P *- None. Roadside parking in Plumley.*

Y *- Bells of Peover, Lower Peover.*

ABOUT THE WALK - A walk in central Cheshire to one of the most attractive churches in the county at Lower Peover. On the way you cross the modern transport route of the M6 and by direct contrast south of Lower Peover follow an old Saltway. From here as you return to Plumley you cross the saltfields, seeing many of the brine pumps. The walk can be extended towards Knutsford adding 4 miles to the walk. The church at Lower Peover, dedicated to St. Oswald, is well worth visiting to see the timbered interior and its many monuments and 700 year old chest.

WALKING INSTRUCTIONS - Starting from the Primitive Methodist church in Plumley at the junction of Trouthall Lane. Turn left along the main road past the Post Office. Just afterwards on your right is the stile and path sign. Turn right and follow the path along the righthand side of the field. At the second stile turn left keeping to the lefthand side of the field to a farm road. Turn right along to Whitehouse Farm. Go straight through to a gate and keep a hedge on your left and reach the perimeter fence of Royd Wood with Tabley Mere beyond. Bear right and for the next 1/2 mile keep the fence on your left. Just after leaving the wood gain a minor lane via a stile and path sign. Turn right and pass a thatched cottage - Parkside Cottage - on your right. Just after turn left at the stile and path sign - Knutsford (Pathsign No. 141). Keep to the lefthand side of the field and in 1/4 mile opposite Parkside Farm cross a footbridge and bear right to the railway underpass. *(The extension route via Knutsford turns left here.)* Go through the underpass and bear right keeping the field edge on your left. At the end of the field reach the farm road close to Diamond Farm on your left.

Turn right along the road and follow it round to your left to a junction. Keep straight ahead past Wash Farm. In 1/4 mile where the road turns right, turn left beside Laurel Cottage, along the No Through Road. Walk through Bucklow Farm and cross the bridge over the M6. Turn right immediately down the steps and walk beside it for 1/4 mile to more steps and Plumley Moor Road. Turn left along the road and walk along it for 1/2 mile to a road junction. Turn right then left along Free Green and in a few yards turn right along Barrows Brow to Lower Peover - inn and church. *(The extension route joins here at Barrows Brow.)*

Turn right at the church through the churchyard to a road and just past the school turn left, as footpath signed. Cross to a kissing gate and continue to a stile. Keep to the righthand side of the field before bearing left to a fenced path which you follow to Fox Covert. Gaining the road here basically go straight across and follow the road round to your right to a junction. Turn left and in a few yards right at the stile and path sign and cross the fields keeping to the lefthandside. Gaining Townfield Lane with Old Mill Farm opposite on your left, cross to your left to a footpath sign. Descend the field to a track lined with trees and cross a footbridge over Bradshaw Brook. Gain Dams Lane - an old saltway and part of The Salter's Way - and follow it to the B5081 road. Turn left and opposite the telephone kiosk in 100 yards turn right and follow the lane - Hulme Hall Lane over the M6. Keep on the track past Hulme Hall over 1/2 mile away and on for another 1/2 mile to a minor road; enroute seeing several brine pumps. At the road turn left then right along Patmos Lane. Follow this to a road junction 1/2 mile away. Turn left and in 100 yards at a footpath sign, turn left. Cross a cattle grid and follow the track keeping to the right and enter woodland to a gate with a house on your left. Continue straight ahead first keeping to the righthand side of the field then lefthand side and cross a bridge over the railway line. Bear right following a defined path to a stile and turn right then left to a stile and lane beside Peover Eye. Turn left along the lane and soon reach Trouthall Lane. Turn left along it past Maltkiln Farm back to the start.

Lower Peover church.

Moat bridge, Hulme Hall.

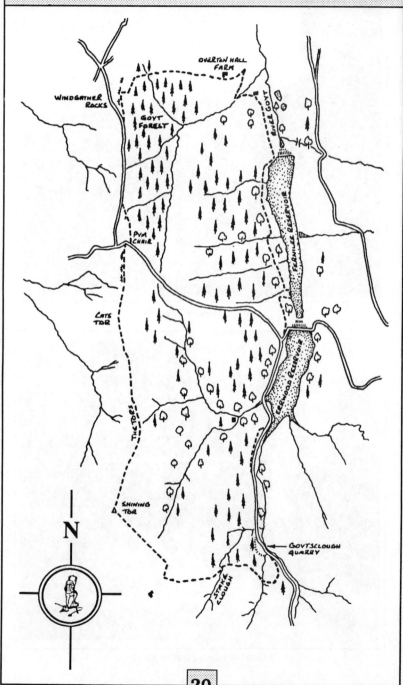

WINDGATHER ROCKS

OVERTON HALL FARM

GOYT FOREST

RIVER GOYT

PYM CHAIR

FERNILEE RESERVOIR

CATS TOR

ERWOOD RESERVOIR

THE TORS

SHINING TOR

GOYTSCLOUGH QUARRY

STAKE CLOUGH

N

THE
GOYT VALLEY
- 10 miles
- allow 4 hours.

= = = *Goytsclough Quarry Car Park—Snake Clough— Shining Tor—The Tors—Cats Tor—Pym Chair —Windgather Rocks— Goyt Forest—Overton Hall Farm— Goyt Valley — Fernilee Reservoir— Erwood Reservoir—Goytsclough Quarry Car Park*

1:25,000 Outdoor Leisure Map—The White Peak - west sheet.

Goytsclough Quarry Car Park. Grid Ref; SK 012734.

- None on the walk; nearest - the Cat & Fiddle Inn 1/2 mile from near Shining Tor.

ABOUT THE WALK - The Goyt Valley, to the west of Buxton, is an exceptionally scenic area with two reservoirs in a moorland setting. This walk takes you through the valley and along its western rim over Shining Tor to Windgather Rocks. The views from the Tor are extensive—to the east the Peak District and westwards the Cheshire Plain. There is a one-way traffic system operating through the Goyt Valley and the only way you can reach Goytsclough Car Park is via Errwood Reservoir.

WALKING INSTRUCTIONS - From the car park walk southwards a short distance to the footpath signposted 'Errwood via Shooters Clough'. The path is a grass track which heads southwards just above the road. Upon reaching the forest 200 yards later, turn right over the ladder stile and follow a distinct path through the trees and across Deep Clough to another wooden ladder stile. You are now walking due west with the trees on your immediate right. Cross Stake Clough and begin ascending with a gritstone wall on your immediate right. The path is well defined and the trees are now behind you. Part way up the hillside ascend the stone stile and keep heading upwards with the wall now on your immediate left. A 1/4 mile later you reach a wide track. Here turn right and soon afterwards left and begin crossing the moorland to the summit of Shining Tor (- 559m. - 1,834 ft.). The actual triangulation pillar is just over the wall.

From the summit turn right, keeping the wall on your left and walk along the crest of the ridge for the next two miles to the road at Pym Chair. The path is well defined all the way as you cross The Tors and Cats Tor (1,703 ft.) . As you walk along you have distant views on all four sides. On reaching the road turn right, then left soon afterwards and cross a 1/4 mile section of grass moorland to the minor road north of the car park. Follow this road for the next 1/2 mile to Windgather Rocks. On nearing the rocks turn right into a very shallow quarry and use the stone stile on the left for the footpath on to the summit of the rocks. Windgather is a very popular climbing ground. About 400 yards along the top of the rocks ascend the wooden ladder stile on your right and follow the fenced path to Goyt Forest. At the end of the wall turn left along the forest edge to another wooden ladder stile. Here turn sharp right and walk through the trees beside a fence to a wall barely 1/4 mile away. Use another ladder stile on your right and leave the trees behind to gain the high point. From here you can look down on to Overton Hall Farm and the Goyt Valley. Descend keeping the forest well to your right, aiming for the track to Overton Hall Farm.

Continue descending down the track, past the farm. Follow the tarmac track as it turns sharp right and descends above Madagascar Farm. Keep to the track as it crosses Mill Clough beyond the angles up the valley side to a house on your left. Bear right and now walk parallel to the Goyt River below along a rough track to the dam wall of Fernilee Reservoir. Upon reaching the road here turn right and shortly afterwards left over a ladder stile to follow the path above the reservoir through the trees to Errwood Car Park and Reservoir, one mile away.

After half a mile there is a junction in the path, keep to the right and ascend slightly to the footbridge across the stream in Deep Clough (another one.) The path now remains level as you continue through the trees catching glimpses of the reservoir. Many ducks, coots and moorhens can be seen on the water. As you near the dam wall of Errwood Reservoir bear right up the path to the road at the top. Continue along the road past the car park on your right with Errwood Reservoir on your left. Goytsclough Quarry car park is 1 1/2 miles away. After half a mile you pass Errwood Hall car park on your right. From here you can take a path through the trees for a third of a mile or alternatively continue up the road to your car park. If you follow the signposted path you return to the road leaving a third of a mile left to the car park. Here your circular walk ends, alas.

Windgather Rocks.

Cat & Fiddle Inn.

SHUTLINGSLOE - 506m.
- 11 MILES

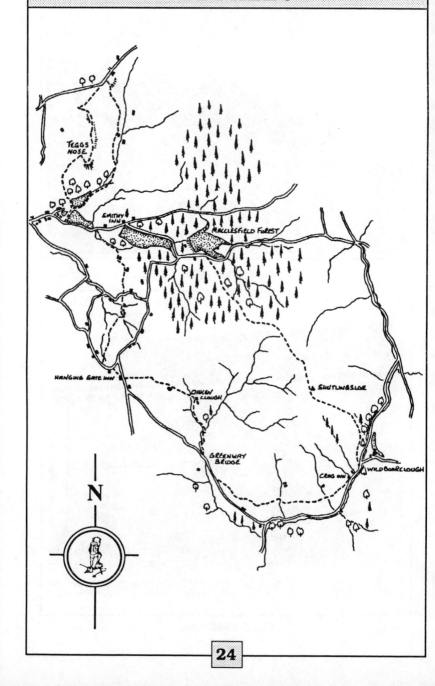

SHUTLINGSLOE
- 506m.
- 11 MILES
- allow 4 hours

Teggs Nose—Bottoms Reservoir, Gritstone Trail — Oaken Clough—Greenway Bridge—Wildboarclough—Shutlingsloe 506m. (1,659 ft.)—Macclesfield Forest—Trentabank Reservoir—Ridgegate Reservoir—Teggs Nose Reservoir—Teggs Nose car park.

1:25,000 Outdoor Leisure Map—The White Peak - west sheet.

Teggs Nose. Grid Ref: SJ 951733.

Crag Inn, Wildboarclough. Hanging Gate Inn. Smithy Inn, just off route.

ABOUT THE WALK - Half the walk is outside the National Park but through really attractive scenery, which will surprise many people who have not walked in this area of Cheshire. For part of the time you follow the Gritstone Trail before crossing into the Peak District to climb the prominent mountain—Shutlingsloe. The route back to your starting point is through Macclesfield and past four reservoirs. Out of all the walks in this book, I think this is one of my all time favourites.

WALKING INSTRUCTIONS - From the car park walk to the road and turn left and follow the Gritstone Trail southwards. The trail is 17 miles long and runs from Lyme Park to Rushton Spencer on the Staffordshire border and was devised by the Cheshire County Council. At the car park is an information office where details about the Trail and other walks can be obtained. The Trail is well marked with yellow discs with a black footprint and the letter 'G'. The direction is indicated by an arrow above the footprint. First you walk along the road a short distance before following a grass track and entering Teggs Nose Country Park. A 1/4 mile later you turn sharp left and walk around the edge of the prominent gritstone outcrops and the quarry. As you walk round you pass several interesting exhibits showing how the quarry operated and what was made here. The southern end has a steep slope and once past this you turn left via a wooden stile and begin descending to the western side of Teggs Nose Reservoir.

After walking along the road in front of this reservoir, go through a gate opposite and walk along the banks of Bottoms Reservoir, keeping first along its western side and then the southern side to a minor road. Continue along the road just past the eastern end of the reservoir and turn right, following the Gritstone Trail, signposted for Croker Hill. For the next 1/4 mile you walk along a track to Greenbarn House. Here you walk around it and continue across the fields, heading south. After crossing three fields, you cross a single track road to a farm. Keep the buildings on your immediate left before beginning to ascend through several fields to the road just south of the hamlet of Fernlee. The whole of this section is well stiled. You now leave the Gritstone Trail and turn left up the road. In 200 yards you come to a signposted path on the right of a house. Don't take this one, but walk past the house and ascend the stone steps on its left-hand side. You now follow a fenced path to the Hanging Gate Inn.

Immediately opposite the inn is a wooden stile and footpath sign— 'Greenway Bridge'. At first you head due east on the left-hand side of a walled track. At the end of the field a 1/4 mile later, turn right and left almost immediately afterwards and begin crossing moorland passing round a small tarn on your right before descending to Oakenclough. The final section to the road at Oakenclough is down a fenced and walled path. As you descend you have splendid views of Shutlingsloe. The true right-of-way goes immediately in front of the house. However, there is an alternative footpath. Upon reaching the road in front of Oakenclough via a wooden stile, turn right and left soon afterwards using a small metal gate and descend to the stream running down Oakenclough. Cross the stream picking up the true right-of-way and descend down the clough keeping the stream on your right all the time to the minor road at Greenway Bridge.

Turn left and walk up the minor road for about 400 yards. Upon reaching the first walled track on your left, turn left and walk along this for a 1/2 mile. At a sharp left-hand bend leave the track via a stone stile and begin crossing the field to the Crag Inn, just south of Wildboarclough. The path line cannot be seen on the ground but all the stiles are there as you cross six fields during the next 3/4 mile. From the inn follow the road towards Wildboarclough but after 200 yards turn left up a tarmac lane and begin ascending towards Shutlingsloe. After 1/4 mile, turn left, as footpath signposted, for Shutlingsloe and Langley. The path is well defined as you begin ascending to the right-hand side of the mountain. On gaining the high ground, a path on your left will bring you to the top and trig point. The effort is well worthwhile, for the view is unsurpassed. Know you can see where you have walked from and what is left to do !

Descend from the summit the way you came up and continue beside the gritstone wall for a short distance before turning left and crossing moorland along a well defined path to Macclesfield Forest. On reaching the forest, turn left along the wide footpath and after 1/4 mile the path bears right and descends through the pine trees to the road above Trentabank Reservoir, 1/2 mile away. At the road turn left and 1/4 mile later bear right to follow the road along the northern side of Ridgegate Reservoir. This is delightful walking. At the north-western end of the reservoir you reach a road junction opposite the Smithy Inn. Turn left down the road rejoining your route earlier in the day beside Bottoms Reservoir. Retrace your steps around this reservoir to the road between Bottoms and Teggsnose Reservoirs. Instead of continuing ahead, turn right and walk along the walled track along the southern side of Teggsnose Reservoir.

About 1/4 mile from the reservoir and indicated by a stone footpath sign on your right, leave the track and cross the stream via stepping stones, and begin heading for the car park. Here, as signposted, you turn left and walk up a walled lane to the car park 1/2 mile away. Before heading home, admire the scene for in the distance you can see Shutlingsloe and can trace much of the way you have walked.

John Merrill walkers on the summit of Shutlingsloe.

TEGG'S NOSE, MACCLESFIELD CANAL & SADDLE OF KERRIDGE - 12 MILES

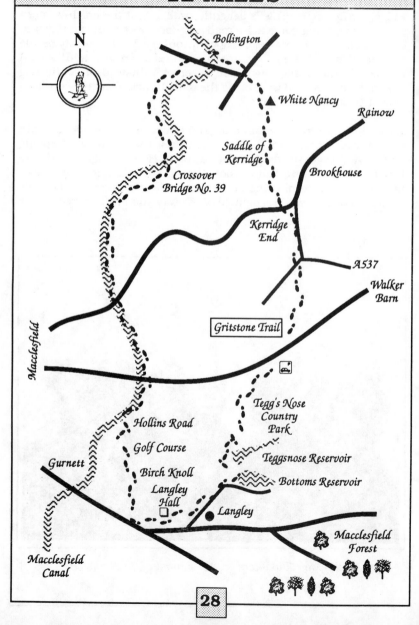

TEGG'S NOSE, MACCLESFIELD CANAL & SADDLE OF KERRIDGE
- 12 MILES
- allow 4 to 5 hours.

- Tegg's Nose Car Park - Tegg's Nose Country Park - Langley - River Bollin - Birch Knoll - The Hollins - Macclesfield Canal - Bollington - White Nancy - Saddle of Kerridge - Trig Point 313m. - Kerridge End - Gritstone Trail - Tegg's Nose Car Park.

- 1:25,000 Pathfinder Series Sheet No. SJ 87/97 - Macclesfield & Alderley Edge.

Tegg's Nose Country Park. Grid Ref. SJ951733

- St. Dunstans Inn, Langley; Puss in Boots, Macclesfield (beside canal); Barge Inn beside the canal, Queens Arms and Red Lion Inn, Bollington.

Refreshments available at Tegg's Nose car park.

ABOUT THE WALK - A mixture of high rugged ridge walking with extensive views to peaceful canal walking at the base of the Pennines. You start at Tegg's Nose and descend to the Macclesfield Canal, which you follow to Bollington. Here you ascend, steeply, to the Saddle of Kerridge and cross high ground back to Tegg's Nose, following part of the Gritstone Trail. The walk makes a nice contrast between remote and densely populated areas. The route is well sprinkled with inns and if you set off about 10.0a.m. you should reach the inns in Bollington before the final ascent!

WALKING INSTRUCTIONS - Starting from the car park return to the road and turn left, along the Gritstone Trail, signposted for Tegg's Nose Summit. Cross two fields to Teggs Nose Country Park and a kissing gate. Through this turn left and keep to the lefthand edge of the quarry working on a wide distinct path. Pass the remains of the early quarry equipment and display area on your left. Where the path divides

and stile. Keep to the righthand side of the field and cross two to a small kissing gate before Bull Hill Lane. Turn right along the lane, gently ascending passing Lower Bull Hill Farm on your right. At the road junction with the A537 road, turn left then right to a stile and path sign; now joint the Gritstone Trail which you follow for the final 3/4 mile back to Tegg's Nose Car Park. The path is well defined as you cross the well stiled fields to the road. Here turn right then left back into the car park.

Quarry machinery - Tegg's Nose.

Langley Hall.

BOSLEY RESERVOIR, CROKER HILL, WINCLE MINN & THE CLOUD - 13 MILES

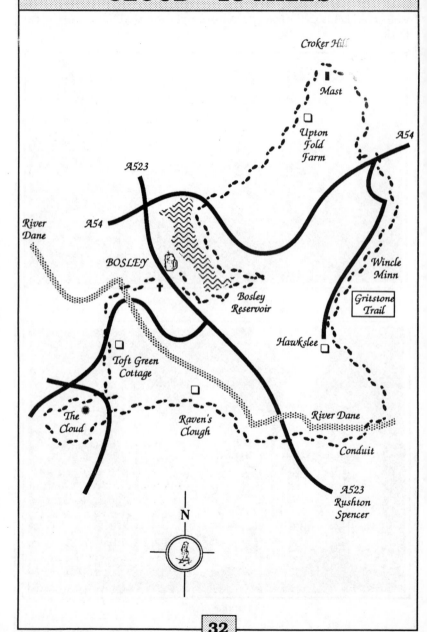

BOSLEY RESERVOIR, CROKER HILL, WINCLE MINN & THE CLOUD - 13 MILES

- allow 5 hours.

- Bosley - Bosley Reservoir - Upton Fold Farm - Croker Hill - Gritstone Trail - Wincle Minn - Hawkslee - Dumkins - Barleigh Ford Bridge - A523 - Raven's Clough - The Cloud, 343m. - Toft Green - Bosley.

1:25,000 Pathfinder Series Sheet No. SJ 86/96 - Congleton.

- No official one. Limited roadside parking near church in Bosley. Grid Ref. 918657.

- Harrington Arms, Queens Arms, Bosley.

ABOUT THE WALK - A high level route along the southern end of the Gritstone Trail. Most of the walk is in Cheshire but in the final part you enter Staffordshire to ascend The Cloud for an unparalleled view over of Cheshire - you can also trace the route you have just done from here! Throughout the walk there are extensive views where you can see the hills giving way to the Cheshire plain. A beautiful walk whatever the season and done clockwise.

WALKING INSTRUCTIONS - Starting from Bosley church, dedicated to St. Mary the Virgin, return to the A523 road and turn right. Pass the Queens Arms and Chaff Hall Farm. Just afterwards turn left at the stile and footpath sign. Cross to a stile and bear right to a gate. Then aim for the earth embankment of Bosley Reservoir where there is a stile. Walk beneath the embankment and ascend the other side to a stile and minor road. Turn left and in a few yards left again and follow the path around the reservoir, heading northwards, for the next mile to the A54 road. Turn right then left and ascend a track - no footpath sign. You ascend to a gate and then keep a fence on your left as you gradually ascend to a barn. Here gain a track and follow it to a stile. You now ascend more steeply guided by stiles and a track to the lefthand side of Upton Fold Farm. Turn right to the farm and follow the track round to your left as you gradually ascend to Croker Hill and its radio mast. Follow the track round to your right to Lingerds Farm, where there is a stile just before it on your left. Turn left - now on the Gritstone Trail - and descend to another stile and onto a track and A54 road.

Turn left then right - Gritstone Trail sign - Barleigh 5 km. (3 miles) - and follow the single track road over Wincle Minn and onto Hawkslee 1 1/2 miles away. The other side of the farm turn left, as signed and descend the righthand side of the fields to woodland. Follow a track to your left and ford Shelf Brook and bear right to pass the ruins of Dumkins. Just after reach a stile and a grass track. Follow this towards Barleighford Farm, but turn right before it, guided by posts, to walk round the righthand side of it to reach Barleigh Ford Bridge. Cross the River Dane and enter Staffordshire. Just after turn right along the water Conduit, as Gritstone Trail signed - Rushton Spencer 1.8 km. Walk beside the conduit for little over 1/2 mile to your third bridge. Here turn right and descend towards the River Dane and a stile. Turn left to cross the field to a stile and the A523 road.

Cross to your left to a footpath sign - Mow Cop Trail and Staffordshire Way. Cross the old railway line to a stile and footbridge over the River Dane. Turn right and walk close to the river then away from it, while it does a large loop, before regaining it and a stile and footbridge over Ravensclough Brook. Turn left and ascend to the right of the brook to Raven's Clough Farm. Turn left at the farm at a stile and follow a track which in 1/4 mile turns right. The right of way on this corner has been rerouted to 150 yards further up the track. Here turn left at the stile and follow the ascending path to your right, which in just over 1/4 mile brings you to road near Hillside Farm beneath The Cloud. Turn left then right up a track, following round to your left to a stile. Over this turn right and keep wall on your right and walk beside Cloud Plantation and in 1/2 mile reach the exposed Cloud Side. Turn right and ascend the path to the triangulation pillar on the summit of The Cloud - 343m.

Follow the path round to your right and descend steps to regain the road near Hillside Farm, you reached here half an hour ago! Turn left and in a few yards right at the stile and descend to another. Continue descending the field to a stile and path sign opposite Toft Green Cottage. Turn left then right along the road towards to Lymford Farm and onto the River Dane, 1/2 mile away. Here re-enter Cheshire and leave the road at the footpath sign - Bosley 1/2 mile. The path is well defined and full of kissing gates and returns you to Bosley church.

WINSFORD & VALE ROYAL - 16 MILES

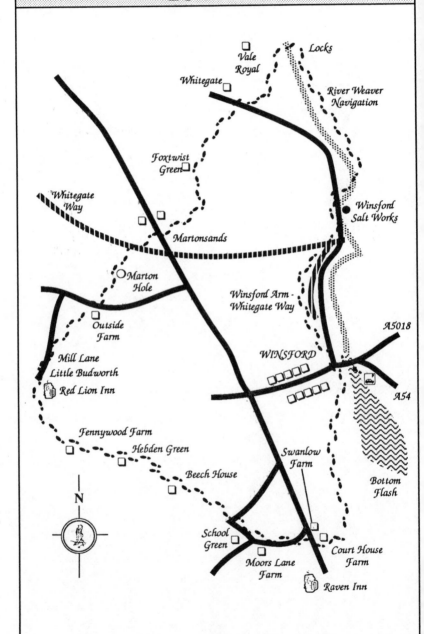

WINSFORD &
VALE ROYAL
- 16 MILES
- allow 6 hours.

▪▪ ▪▪ ▪▪ - *Winsford - Bottom Flash - Court House Farm - Moors Lane Farm - School Green - Beech House - Hebden Green - Fennywood Farm - Lower Farm - Little Budworth - Congreaves Farm - Outside Farm - Marton Hole - Whitegate Way - Martonsands - Beauty Bank - Foxtwist Green - Whitegate - Vale Royal - Locks - Weaver Navigation - Valeroyal Cut - Meadowbank - Whitegate Way (Winsford arm) - Winsford.*

1:25,000 Pathfinder Series Sheet No. 775 (SJ 66/76) - Winsford (Cheshire) and Sandbach.
- Sheet No. 758 (SJ 67/77) - Northwich & Knutsford.

- Beside Bottom Flash, just off the A54. Grid Ref. 656663.

- Several in Winsford including - The Ark Inn & Vale Royal Arms. Raven Inn, Swanlow Lane. Red Lion Inn, Little Budworth - 1/2 way point! Inn at Beauty Bank.

ABOUT THE WALK - A walk in the heart of Cheshire in the Vale Royal district. The first half to Little Budworth follows little used rights of way. But from this attractive village the walk changes to being outstanding. First is Marton Hole then onto the Whitegate Way before weaving your way through fields and hamlets to Valeroyal Park. Here you gain the fascinating locks of the Weaver Navigation before walking beside it towards Winsford. A great area for bird watching with curlew in the fields and a kingfisher on the river. You pass a salt mine before picking up the Winsford arm of the Whitegate Way and return to Winsford.

WALKING INSTRUCTIONS - From the car park walk over the road bridge and turn left and follow the path close to the shore of Bottom Flash. Gain a stile at the end of the houses on your right and continue across a field ascending slightly to your right to gain a stile and path sign on the edge of the caravans of Thornley Weaver Park. Walk to the shop and turn right up the track. In a few yards turn left and follow another track and follow it for 1/4 mile. You cross a wooded area with stream on your right and 20 yards later turn right at a "stile". Ascend

37

and cross the field to its far righthand corner where there is a stile. Turn left following a grass track to the farm track at Weavergrove Farm. Turn right along this track, following it round to your left. In 1/4 mile pass woodland on your left and a stream on your right. Ascend slightly before leaving the track and aiming for the top righthand corner of the field where there is a stile/gate. Keep the hedge on your right to the next gate/stile and continue ahead to another gate. Turn right and follow a concrete drive to the B5074 road, near Court House Farm.

Turn right along Swanlow Lane - Raven Inn is just to your left. Follow the road for more than 1/4 mile and just after Swanlow Farm on your right, turn left along Moors Lane. Follow it for 1/2 mile to School Green. Where the road turns right at Knobs Cottage, take the track on its left. Keep on this for 1/2 mile to Beech House. Continue past the house to a gate and footpath sign. Keep the hedge on your right and 1/4 mile from the house reach another track with Woodford Hall just ahead. Turn right to Hebden Green and house dated 1876. Reaching the road here turn left on the track and pass Woodford Hall. 1/2 mile later reach Fennywood Farm. Entering the farm turn right to a gate and continue to another. The next field is over 1/4 mile wide but you will see Little Budworth ahead. Aim towards it and the middle of the field to a stile and hedge. Continue with the hedge on your left and the path soon becomes a track leading to Well Lane, lower Farm and Little Budworth. Gain the road in the village opposite the church; to your left is the Red Lion Inn.

Turn right along Mill Lane, from the church, and keep on it for 1/2 mile to a footpath sign and drive to a house on your right. Turn right along the drive for a few yards to a stile on your left. Cross the field to the right of Coneygreaves Farm to a stile. Turn right with the hedge on your right and pass Grange Farm on your right and onto the A54 road. Turn right and in 50 yards opposite Outside Farm turn left - footpath signed Marton Hole. Bear right to a gate before descending the field to a bridge over Shay's Lane Brook. Ascend to a stile and continue to another before keeping the hedge on your left and Marton Hole on your right. Continue across the field aiming for the left of Marton Hall, to a stile, picnic table and Whitegate Way. Turn right then left and descend the track to the road at Martonsands. Cross to your right to a stile and footpath sign - "Beauty Bank." The path is well signed as you walk round to your right before ascending to your left to a track. Turn right and reach the road at Beauty Bank - there is an inn to your left. Turn left then right, as footpath signed -Foxtwist Green. At first keep the hedge on your left then descend to a footbridge before ascending to Foxtwist Green.

Turn right then left at the footpath sign and walk on the righthand side of Swallows Nest. Continue along the field edge before descending to a footbridge over Pettypool Brook. Ascend to a gate and the road at

Whitegate. Cross to Mill Lane and ascend the road round to your right to a stile and footpath sign Vale Royal Lock. You now follow a track across a field to the edge of woodland, which you walk beside before turning right into it, where you turn left to walk through it to a stile. Turn right and soon left along the field edge to more woodland. Beside the wood turn right - now a well defined path - and reach the banks of the River Weaver. Turn left and walk along the banks of the river to the drive to Vale Royal on your left. Continue on the drive to small parking area on your right. Turn right and follow the drive over a footbridge and onto Vale Royal Locks.

Over the locks turn right - history notes are on the notice board - and follow the well defined path along Vale Royal Cut. In a mile reach New Bridge Picnic area. Turn right across the navigation to the road. (It is feasible to continue along the river all the way to Winsford.) Turn left along the road past the Winsford Salt Works on your left and in 1/2 mile reach the Whitegate Way on your right. Turn right then left along the Winsford arm and follow the way for 2/3 mile to the Winsford Terminus. Turn right along the road into Winsford and on the otherside of the large roundabout is the car park where you began.

Vale Royal Locks on the River Weaver Navigation.

DELAMERE FOREST
& HELSBY HILL - 13 MILES

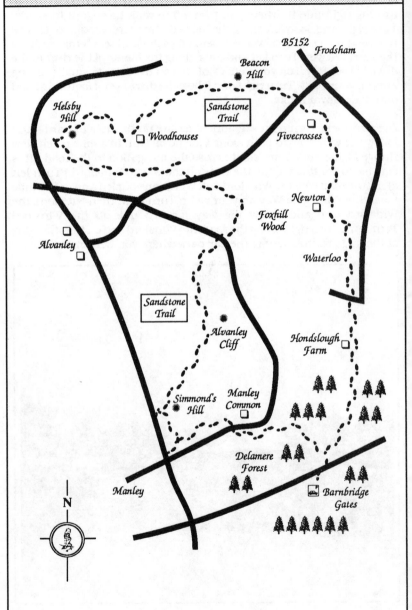

B5152 Frodsham

Beacon Hill

Helsby Hill

Sandstone Trail

Woodhouses

Fivecrosses

Newton

Foxhill Wood

Alvanley

Waterloo

Sandstone Trail

Alvanley Cliff

Hondslough Farm

Simmond's Hill

Manley Common

Delamere Forest

Manley

Barnbridge Gates

N

DELAMERE FOREST & HELSBY HILL
- 13 MILES
- allow 4 1/2 hours.

Barnbridge Gates, Delamere Forest - Waterloo - Depmore - Newton - Fivecrosses - Beacon Hill - Sandstone Trail - Woodhouse - Helsby Hill - Sandstone Trail - Alvanley Cliff - Simmond's Hill - Manley Common - Delamere Forest - Barnbridge Gates.

- 1:25,000 Pathfinder Series Sheet No. 757 (SJ 47/57) - Ellesmere Port (East).

- Barnbridge Gates, Delamere Forest. Grid Ref. 543715.

- One just off the route at Fivecrosses.

ABOUT THE WALK - A beautiful walk starting from the forest and heading north to the Sandstone Trail and Helsby Hill. Here are extensive views over the Mersey. You rejoin the Sandstone Trail and follow it back to the forest where you began.

WALKING INSTRUCTIONS - From Barnbridge Gate car park, cross the road to a track and Sandstone Trail. Bear right along the track and in a few yards the Sandstone Trail turns left - this is you return route. Continue ahead, ignoring all side tracks and in 1/4 mile reach a marshy area on your right. Continue to the forest perimeter where there is a stile. Bear left along the edge of the field to a stile and track. Continue on the track past Pinewood Farm. Just after keep straight ahead, as footpath signed - "Waterloo" - and keep on the track along the edge of woodland. Follow it round to your left around another marshy/wooded area and almost encircle it to reach a stile and footpath sign. Go over the stile and continue on a track to the bend in Waterloo Lane. Keep on the lane for the next 3/4 mile; ignoring all side road until Depmore. Soon pass the houses of Waterloo and 1/4 mile later Marl Pits on your left. Nearly 1/2 mile later a five-way junction at Depmore.

Bear left; not sharp left, along the road towards Fivecrosses. After 100 yards just past a haulage firm on your left is a stile and footpath sign.

Turn left along the field edge to another stile, where turn right and keep the hedge on your right. In 1/4 mile reach the road opposite the Hilltop Equestrian Centre. Turn right then left along a track with a house on your left and keep to the righthand side of the fields for the next 1/2 mile. Pass through several gates before reaching a stile and track. Follow this to a road and bear left. In a few yards it divides - to your right at the end of the road is an inn at Fivecrosses. Turn left then right along a small road between the houses. Follow it for 1/4 mile to house No. 24. Go over the stile by the path sign. Walk along the field edge past a small play area and swings before turning left and ascending the field edge to a stile. Turn right at the top and follow the path round to your right and descend with sandstone caves on your left. At the bottom reach a road. Turn left then right along the road to Mersey View and Frodsham Golf Course. 1/4 mile along here is the car park and start of the Sandstone Trail at Beacon Hill.

Just past the car park turn left at the trail sign and descend across the golf course to the top of a gorge and woodland. Turn left and descend the steps to the base of Jacob's Ladder - the more adventurous can descend directly down the "sandstone ladder." At the bottom is a Mid Cheshire Footpath Society sign. Here you leave the Sandstone Trail, which now goes left over Woodhouse Hill. Turn right and follow the wide path beneath the sandstone cliffs to a wall on your left with steps. Turn left over the steps and descend and for the next 1/2 mile keep to the outer edge of the woodland to a kissing gate. Turn right and walk along the drive from The Holt to Tarvin Road. Turn left then right and walk along Chestnut Lane to a ford. Cross it and ascend steps to a stile. Follow the path beyond to a hedged path. Keep ahead to a stile and continue to another and reach Bates Lane. Turn right along it and turn left along Old Chester Road. In a few yards on the right of Holly Cottage is a footpath sign and stile. Ascend to another and onto another on your right at the edge of woodland. Turn right entering National Trust property. Keep to the upper path and soon keep left and start ascending to the summit of Helsby Hill.

From the triangulation pillar turn left along the path to a stile and track. Turn left and pass Hammerslake Farm on your left. Continue on the lane following round to a stile and pathsign 1/4 mile away - "Tarvin Road, Commonside." Soon reach a ladder stile and bear left and reach a stile in the bottom righthand corner of the field. Follow the path to a road, opposite mobile homes. Turn left down the road for a few yards to a stile and footpath sign. Turn right and keep to the edge of the field to Burrows Lane. Turn left to a road with Foxhill Wood infront. Turn right and in a few yards you are back on the Sandstone Trail, for the remainder of the walk - approx 4 miles - you are following the trail.

Walk along the road for 1/4 mile to Ridgeway Wood. Turn right up the steps following the path signs - Manley Common and Delamere Forest.

Follow the path around the wood and down the lefthand side of a field to the road at Commonside. Cross over and continue along the lefthand side of the fields with Alvanley Cliff on your left. Well after the second stile from the road the path turns right then left to gain a lane. Cross this and continue on the trail to Manley Road. Turn right then left and walk along the road beneath Simmond's Hill. Keep on the road for 1/2 mile passing St. John's church on your left, to the road junction with Pingot Lane. Turn left at the stile and path sign, following the path, which soon bears right to the road at Manley Common. Turn left along the road to the lefthand bend in the road. Here take the second path on your left and follow a track into Delamere Forest. Entering the forest the track bears right and upon meeting another turn left. In 1/2 mile turn right then left and follow the track close to the edge of the forest for a short distance before swinging right and gaining your starting out path, Retrace your steps back to Barnbridge Gates car park. The Sandstone Trail is well signed and waymarked. One most stiles is a yellow disc with a boot sole with the letter S. An arrow indicates the direction of travel. Alas, here in the forest the walk ends. The walk from Beeston Castle follows another section of the trail.

Helsby crag.

43

BEESTON, BICKERTON HILL &
THE SANDSTONE TRAIL
- 14 MILES

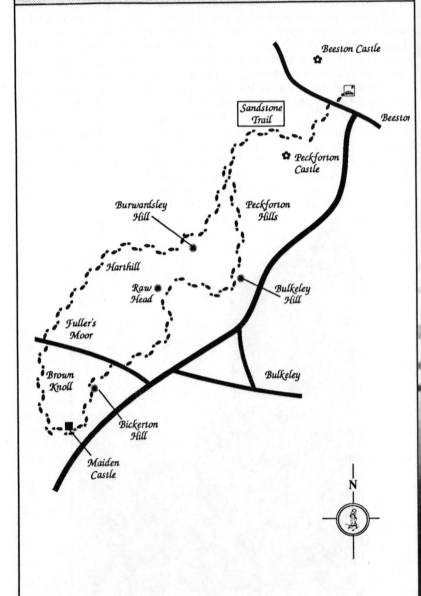

BEESTON, BICKERTON HILL & THE SANDSTONE TRAIL
- 14 MILES
- allow 5 or more hours.

- Beeston Castle - Moathouse Farm - Willow Hill - Burwardsley - Burwardsley Hill - Mickerloo Farm - Harthill - Fuller's Moor - Brown Knoll - Maiden Castle - Bickerton Hill - Sandstone Trail - Raw Head - Bulkeley Hill - Peckforton Hills - Moathouse Farm - Beeston Castle.

O.S. MAP *- 1:25,000 Pathfinder Series Sheet No.790 (SJ 45/55) - Farndon, Holt and Tattenhall.*

- Beeston Castle, Grid Ref. 540589.

- None on the walk; nearest - The Bickerton Poacher, 1/2 mile from route. Inn on the A534 road at Fuller's Moor, 100 yards from route. Tea and refreshments at car park.

ABOUT THE WALK - Outstanding! The Sandstone Trail between Beeston Castle and Maiden Castle is exceptional with woodland and sandstone cliffs. The area around Raw Head is unsurpassed. This walk takes you around the western side of the trail passing other wood and craggy hills to Brown Knoll. From here you ascend onto the trail and follow it northwards back to Beeston Castle and its Sandstone Trail car park. You walk more than a mile of the trail at the start and retrace it as you return, but this only adds to the enjoyment of the walk!

WALKING INSTRUCTIONS - Turn left out of the car park onto the Sandstone Trail. First it along a track by the perimeter wall of the castle. But in a few yards you turn left and descend through the pine trees to a road. Cross to your left and continue along the trail across the field to a footbridge. Ascend the otherside to a lane near Moathouse Farm. Turn right, passing the farm and in 1/4 mile turn left on the trail, signposted Bulkeley Hill. Keep on the track at the base of the hills and

45

woodland for 3/4 mile. Where the trail turns left and ascends keep on the track. You will be returning to here in little over 12 miles time!

Continue on the track to a gate and follow a lane for little over 1/4 mile. Take the first walled track on your right and descend to a road. Turn left and ascend to a road junction near Willow Hill. Turn right then left and walk beneath the hill and in 1/4 mile pass a Field Centre on your right and church dedicated to St. John. Keep right on the road just afterwards and in 80 yards turn left along Harthill Road. In 1/4 mile walk along the base of Cawley's Wood and Burwardsley Hill. Pass Mickerra Farm and immediately afterwards Mickerloo Farm. Here turn left for the signed path Harthill. Keep to the righthand side of the field and descend and ascend to a stile. Continue ascending to the righthand side of Bodnick Wood where there is a stile. Walk beside it for a few yards before turning right and descending along the field edge to a hedged track - Garden Lane. Gaining the road in Harthill, turn right then left along The Green, following a track, signposted "Brown Knoll". The track passes a farm and keeps close to woodland on your left - Park Wood. Where the wood turns sharp left leave it and walk beside a hedge on your left as you descend to a stile on your left. Turn left over it and gain a footbridge. Cross this and walk beside a hedge on your left to the A534 road. Turn left then right along Smithy Lane. There is an inn 100 yards to your left on the A534 road.

Walk along the lane keeping straight ahead at all junctions to reach the Methodist church in Brown Knoll. Just after the road turns sharp right. Keep straight ahead on Lower Sandy Lane. Where it turns sharp left, turn right along the track to another beside a house. Turn left along it to a small National Trust car park. Turn left along a track in woodland following it round and up to a saddle on the right of Maiden Castle. Here you are back on the Sandstone Trail, which you follow all the way back to Beeston Castle. Turn left and ascend the trail and steps to the Maiden Castle - a former Iron Age Fort. Turn left along the edge of the hill, with the drop on your left. Pass the plaque to Larkton Hill and in 1/2 mile near Mad Allen's Hole is a large sandstone boulder with inscriptions "To Kitty." The trail now descends to a road. Turn left and pass Holy Trinity church on your right. Cross the road beyond and walk along Brunty Bank to a road junction on your left. Bear left and ascend - trail signed Raw Head. Along the road to your right is the Bickerton Poacher Inn, 1/2 mile away.

The trail soon swings left as you walk through woodland to Musket's Hole, 1/2 mile away. Here the grandeur of the sandstone cliffs are at their best. Follow the path round and ascend steps to the summit of Raw Head. Continue on the trail curving round to your right and reaching a lane. 1/4 mile along it reach the stile and pathsign - Bulkeley Hill. Follow the path beyond and turn left then right and ascend through woodland to a small reservoir on your left. Keep the

Sandstone Trail sign.

edge of the hill on your right and follow the basically level path to the top of the hill. Follow the path onwards and slowly descend, bearing left at the bottom and descend steps to a track. Turn right along it then left and right again on the track, signed Beeston Castle. The path soon becomes a sunken one, with woodland on your right. 1/4 mile later reach a lane. Turn left then right at Rock Cottage. Where the lane bears left turn right at the stile and path sign and enter woodland. In 1/4 mile you descend to you starting out path. Turn right and follow the track back to Moathouse Farm - retracing your outward route. Walk along the road and turn left across the fields back to Beeston Castle where you began, earlier in the day.

Sandstone cliffs near Raw Head.

SHROPSHIRE UNION CANAL - 15 MILES

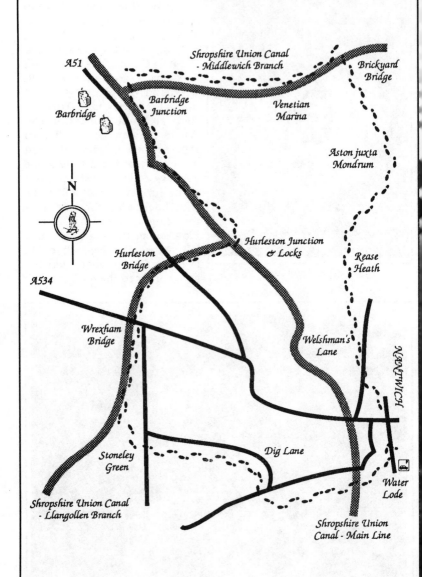

SHROPSHIRE UNION CANAL
- 15 MILES
- allow 5 to 6 hours.

■● ●■ ■● *Nantwich - Manor House Farm - Dig Lane - Stoneley Green - Llangollen Branch - Hurleston Junction - Main Line - Barbridge Junction - Middlewich Branch - Brickyard Bridge - Aston juxta Mondrum - Rease Heath - Welshmen's Lane - Nantwich.*

 - 1:25,000 Pathfinder Sheet No. 791 (SJ65/75) - Crewe.

 off Water Lode road.

Numerous in Nantwich. Two approximately halfway along the route, but on the otherside of the canal! - Barbridge Inn and Jolly Tar Inn, Barbridge. Teas at Venetian Marina.

ABOUT THE WALK - A superb canal walk walking sections of the Shropshire Union Canal - Main Line, Llangollen branch and Middlewich branch. To reach the canal you follow an attractive lane to Stoneley Green. To return from the northern end of the walk you traverse fields following little used rights of way. Nantwich has many attractive buildings and well worth exploring - as you re-enter Nantwich you pass several. The walk is done clockwise. The canals are popular with fishermen seeking roach, chubb and dace.

WALKING INSTRUCTIONS - From the car park on Water Lode road, turn right out of it and follow the road round to your right, for 150 yards to the River Weaver, footbridge and granite boulder on your left. The boulder is 400 million years old. Turn left over the bridge and follow the tarmaced path to your left and over another footbridge. Follow the path on the immediate left of the houses to Queens Drive. Bear left along it and in 1/4 mile keep straight ahead on the road to the bridge over the Main Line of the Shropshire Union Canal. Continue along the road - Marsh Lane, passing Manor House Farm, then Moss Cottage. Shortly after turn right into Dig Lane. Follow this round to your left and keep straight ahead for the next mile. At the second crossroads go straight across and follow the No Through Road through Stoneley Green. At the end of the houses follow the track round to your right to a gate - ahead can be seen Butcher's Bridge. Walk beside the field hedge on your left for a few yards and where it turns left keep straight ahead to a stile and the Llangollen Branch of the canal.

Turn right and keep the canal on your left. Follow the towpath for the next three miles to the flight locks leading down to Hurleston Junction. Cross the footbridge over the Main Line of the canal and turn left. Follow this canal for the next 1 1/2 miles to Barbridge Junction. Almost at the junction is the Barbridge Inn and 1/4 mile later is the Jolly Tar Inn; both of which can be reached via canal bridges. At the junction cross the bridge just before it and reach the towpath of the Middlewich Branch. Turn right along it, now keeping the canal on your right. After nearly 2 miles pass the Venetian Marina on your right (teas). Continue on the canal for nearly a mile to the next bridge - Brickyard Bridge. The bridge has collapsed but there is a wooden footbridge across it.

Cross the bridge to your right to a stile. Keep the field boundary on your left and after 1/2 mile gain a track. Follow this, still on the lefthand side of the fields to the bridge over the railway near Aston Hall. Cross the bridge and turn left through the stile and reach Dairy Lane in Aston juxta Mondrum. Cross over and continue along a road and at the T junction turn right and pass the school on your left. Just after keep straight ahead on Church Road, past the church dedicated to St. Oswald. Opposite the last house - Hillcrest - turn left through the stile. In a few yards reach another and leave the field edge and cross to the far righthand side, using a small electric pylon as a guide. Near it is a footbridge. Cross the next field to another and a stile beyond. Turn left along the field edge to gain the lane close to Poole Old Hall.

Turn right along the lane and in 1/4 mile is a stile and path sign on your right. There should be one on your left but there is nothing. I have traced the line of the path to Poole Hall - found two stiles and a lot of barbed wire! Instead - unless there is now a stile and path sign - continue on the lane to a T junction. Turn left and in little over 1/4 mile on the otherside of small "valley" is a stile and path sign on your left. Turn left and cross the lefthand side of the field to another stile and gain Rease Heath. Gaining the road there turn right - Cinder Lane. Follow it to a T junction and turn left. Follow the road - Wettonhall Road - round the impressive Reasenath Old Hall to the A51 road. Go straight across and follow Welshmen's Lane for 1/2 mile passing the Police Dog Training School on your right and Henhull Hall Farm on your left. Ahead can be seen the Main Line of the Shropshire Union Canal. Approximately 140 yards from the farm on your left is a stile by a gate.

Turn left and keep to the lefthand edge of the field to another stile. Continue by the hedge to another stile and footbridge. Keep the hedge on your right as you ascend slightly and over the "hill" gain Red Lion Lane. Turn right along it inbetween the houses to the A534 road beside the Wilbraham Arms. Turn left towards central Nantwich passing several attractive buildings. Cross the River Weaver and turn right along Water Lode. Soon you reach the Glacier boulder and monument plaque to the great fire of Nantwich in 1583/4. Retrace your steps back to the car park.

Nantwich Fire Plaque.

Glacial boulder.

Hurleston Junction - last lock.

MARBURY & GRINDLEY BROOK
- 12 MILES

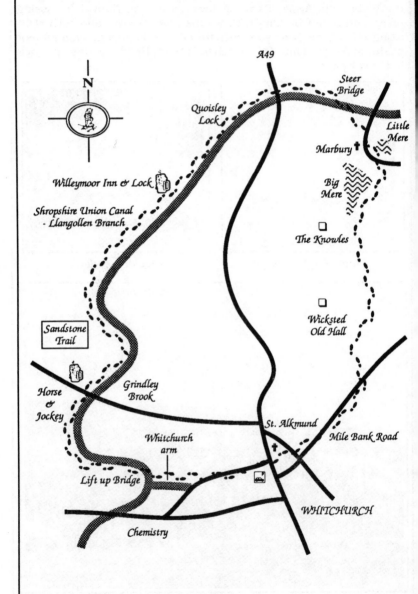

MARBURY &
GRINDLEY BROOK
- 12 MILES
- allow 4 to 5 hours.

━━ ・━ ━━ *- Whitchurch - Mile Bank Farm - Peel's Gorse - Big Wood - Big Mere - Marbury - Steer Bridge - Llangollen Branch of the Shropshire Union Canal - Sandstone Trail - Grindley Brook - Whitchurch.*

1:25,000 Pathfinder Series Sheet No. 807 (SL 44/54) - Whitchurch (Shropshire) and Malpas (Cheshire).

- Central Whitchurch, near St. Alkmund church.

- Numerous in Whitchurch including Greyhound Inn, Horse & Jockey, and Black Bear Inn. Swan Inn, Marbury. Willeymoor Inn at Willeymoor Lock on the canal. Horse & Jockey Inn, Grindley Brook.

ABOUT THE WALK - You start in Shropshire from the attractive town of Whitchurch. First you follow little used rights of way to Big Mere and Marbury. Together they are the prettiest sight in Cheshire. The church tower has suffered from subsidence and is now 27 inches out of line! A mile from the village you gain the Llangollen branch, which you follow for nearly six miles, picking up the southern end of the Sandstone Trail. You regain the town of Whitchurch via the abandoned canal arm that was closed in 1949. Whitchurch is well worth exploring and St Alkmund's church is a magnificent Georgian building. The walk is done anti-clockwise.

WALKING INSTRUCTIONS - Starting from from St. Alkmund church in Whitchurch, turn right along the lane beside it, on the left of the Black Bear Inn. Pass the Horse & Jockey Inn and at the end of the road go straight across and follow Claypit Street. In 2/3 mile pass a cemetery on your left. 100 yards later on your left is a gate. Cross the corner of the field to the second gate and cross the field to a stile on your left. Keep a wooden fence on your right and keep to the right of a couple of ponds to a gate. Descend to your left to a stile and step into Cheshire.

Ascend gently keeping to the lefthand side of Peel's Gorse (woodland) and gain a stile. Continue ahead to another stile with Wicksted Old Hall on your left. Cross the next field to a gate near a pond. Here you descend slightly to a stile before keeping the hedge on your right; on your left is Big Wood. Walk beneath a small hill and descend Buttermilk Bank to a stile close to woodland on your right and on your left is The Knowles. The path is now well defined as you walk beside the woodland and onto the banks of Big Mere. Ahead can be seen Marbury's church dedicated to St. Michael. Partway round the mere leave it and bear right to a gate and footpath sign.

Turn left through the village, passing the Swan Inn on your right. Follow the road round to your left with the church drive on your left. Just after is road junction - School Lane on your right. On your left is a path sign and stile. The path is well stiled and in a 1/3 mile gain Wirswall Road. Turn left and in a few yards right at the footpath signed - "Canal". Keep to the immediate left of Hadley Covert, guided by stiles and just after gain the road close to Steer Bridge and the canal. Cross the bridge and turn left and gain the canal. Keep the canal on your left for almost 6 miles to near Chemistry. In more than a mile pass Quoisley Lock and after 2 miles Willeymoor Inn and Lock. Here you join the Sandstone Trail. Continue along the canal past Povey's Lock and in another 1 1/2 miles reach Grindley Brook and its locks. Continue on the canal for almost another mile. Pass under Danson's Bridge No. 30 then onto 30A. 1/4 mile later is New Mills Liftup Bridge. Here cross the canal and follow the line of the Whitchurch Arm; plans are afoot to restore part of it. Keep to the lefthand side and gain a lane which leads to a road. Turn left along it and in 1/2 mile you are back at St. Alkmund's church.

Big Mere & Marbury church.

Quoisley Lock.

Approaching Grindley Brook.

WALK RECORD CHART

Date walked.

LAMALOAD RESERVOIR & LYME PARK - 15 MILES..............

PRESTBURY & ALDERLEY EDGE - 13 MILES ....

PLUMLEY & LOWER PEOVER - 11 MILES ....

THE GOYT VALLEY - 10 MILES ....

SHUTLINGSLOE - 11 MILES ....

TEGG'S NOSE, MACCLESFIELD CANAL & SADDLE OF

KERRIDGE - 12 MILES ....

BOSLEY RESERVOIR, CROKER HILL, WINCLE MINN & THE

CLOUD - 13 MILES ....

WINSFORD & VALE ROYAL - 16 MILES ....

DELAMERE FOREST & HELSBY HILL - 13 MILES ....

BEESTON, BICKERTON HILL & THE SANDSTONE TRAIL -

14 MILES ....

SHROPSHIRE UNION CANAL - 15 MILES ....

MARBURY & GRINDLEY BROOK - 12 MILES ....

THE JOHN MERRILL WALK BADGE

Complete six of the walks in this book and get the above special John Merrill walk badge and signed certificate. Badges are blue cloth with walking man in four colours and lettering embroidered in blue and measure 3 1/2" in diameter.

BADGE ORDER FORM

Date and details of walks completed..

....

NAME ....

ADDRESS ....

....

Price: £2.75 each including postage, VAT and signed completion certificate.
Amount enclosed (Payable to Trail Crest Publications) ..

From: **TRAIL CREST PUBLICATIONS Ltd.,**
Winster, Matlock, Derbyshire. DE4 2DQ.
✆ **/Fax** (0629) 826354 - 24hr answering service.

************* **YOU MAY PHOTOCOPY THIS FORM** *********
"I'VE DONE A JOHN MERRILL WALK" T SHIRT -
Emerald Green with white lettering and walking man logo. Send £7.50 to Trail Crest Publications stating size required.
John Merrill's "Happy Walking!" Cap - £2.50

Walk the
SALTER'S WAY

The Salter's Way follows an ancient saltway from the heart of Cheshire salt country - Northwich. The 25 1/2 mile route starts beside a canal and weaves its way across the Cheshire Plain past historical buildings and Jodrell Bank Radio Telescope to the Macclesfield Canal. Here the level section ends with the climb into the Pennines to the walks end close to the Cheshire/Derbyshire boundary at Saltersford. The walk is a challenge to complete in a day but makes an excellent two day hike from the plains to the Pennines. A certificate and badge are available for the successful!

see John Merrill's guide to the walk!

EQUIPMENT NOTES
.... some personal thoughts

BOOTS - *preferably with a full leather upper, of medium weight, with a vibram sole. I always add a foam cushioned insole to help cushion the base of my feet.*

SOCKS - *I generally wear two thick pairs as this helps minimise blisters. The inner pair are of loop stitch variety and approximately 80% wool. The outer are a thick rib pair of approximately 80% wool.*

WATERPROOFS - *for general walking I wear a T shirt or cotton shirt with a cotton wind jacket on top. You generate heat as you walk and I prefer to layer my clothes to avoid getting too hot. Depending on the season will dictate how many layers you wear. In soft rain I just use my wind jacket for I know it quickly dries out. In heavy or consistant rain I slip on a neoprene lined cagoule, and although hot and clammy it does keep me reasonably dry. Only in extreme conditions will I don overtrousers, much preferring to get wet and feel comfortable. I never wear gaiters!*

FOOD - *as I walk I carry bars of chocolate, for they provide instant energy and are light to carry. In winter a flask of hot coffee is welcome. I never carry water and find no hardship from not doing so, but this is a personal matter! From experience I find the more I drink the more I want and sweat. You should always carry some extra food such as Kendal Mint Cake, for emergencies.*

RUCKSACKS - *for day walking I use a climbing rucksack of about 40 litre capacity and although it leaves excess space it does mean that the sac is well padded, with an internal frame and padded shoulder straps. Inside apart from the basics for one day I carry gloves, balaclava, spare pullover and a pair of socks.*

MAP & COMPASS - *when I am walking I always have the relevant map - preferably 1:25,000 scale - open in my hand. This enables me to constantly check that I am walking the right way. In case of bad weather I carry a compass, which once mastered gives you complete confidence in thick cloud or mist.*

"from footprint to finished book"

OTHER BOOKS by John N. Merrill Published by TRAIL CREST PUBLICATIONS Ltd.

LAKELAND CHALLENGE WALK
THE RUTLAND WATER CHALLENGE WALK
MALVERN HILLS CHALLENGE WALK
THE SALTER'S WAY
THE SNOWDON CHALLENGE
CHARNWOOD FOREST CHALLENGE WALK
THREE COUNTIES CHALLENGE WALK (Peak District).

INSTRUCTION & RECORD -
HIKE TO BE FIT.....STROLLING WITH JOHN
THE JOHN MERRILL WALK RECORD BOOK

MULTIPLE DAY WALKS -
THE RIVERS'S WAY
PEAK DISTRICT: HIGH LEVEL ROUTE
PEAK DISTRICT MARATHONS
THE LIMEY WAY
THE PEAKLAND WAY

COAST WALKS & NATIONAL TRAILS -
ISLE OF WIGHT COAST PATH
PEMBROKESHIRE COAST PATH
THE CLEVELAND WAY

PEAK DISTRICT HISTORICAL GUIDES -
A to Z GUIDE OF THE PEAK DISTRICT
DERBYSHIRE INNS - an A to Z guide
HALLS AND CASTLES OF THE PEAK DISTRICT & DERBYSHIRE
TOURING THE PEAK DISTRICT & DERBYSHIRE BY CAR
DERBYSHIRE FOLKLORE
PUNISHMENT IN DERBYSHIRE
CUSTOMS OF THE PEAK DISTRICT & DERBYSHIRE
WINSTER - a souvenir guide
ARKWRIGHT OF CROMFORD
LEGENDS OF DERBYSHIRE
TALES FROM THE MINES by Geoffrey Carr
PEAK DISTRICT PLACE NAMES by Martin Spray

JOHN MERRILL'S MAJOR WALKS -
TURN RIGHT AT LAND'S END
WITH MUSTARD ON MY BACK
TURN RIGHT AT DEATH VALLEY
EMERALD COAST WALK

SKETCH BOOKS -
SKETCHES OF THE PEAK DISTRICT

OVERSEAS GUIDES -
HIKING IN NEW MEXICO - Vol I - The Sandia and Manzano Mountains.
Vol 2 - Hiking "Billy the Kid" Country.
"WALKING IN DRACULA COUNTRY" - Romania.
IN PREPARATION -
SHORT CIRCULAR WALKS IN EAST STAFFORDSHIRE
SHORT CIRCULAR WALKS IN THE AMBER VALLEY (DERBYSHIRE).

REMEMBER
AND
OBSERVE
THE
COUNTRY
CODE

Enjoy the countryside and respect its life and work.

Guard against all risk of fire.

Fasten all gates.

Keep your dogs under close control.

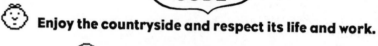 Keep to public paths across farmland.

Use gates and stiles to cross fences, hedges and walls.

Leave livestock, crops and machinery alone.

Take your litter home - pack it in; pack it out.

Help to keep all water clean.

Protect wildlife, plants and trees.

Take special care on country roads

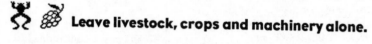

Make no unnecessary noise.

THE HIKER'S CODE

✿ *Hike only along marked routes - do not leave the trail.*

✿ *Use stiles to climb fences; close gates.*

✿ *Camp only in designated campsites.*

✿ *Carry a light-weight stove.*

✿ *Leave the trail cleaner than you found it.*

✿ *Leave flowers and plants for others to enjoy.*

✿ *Keep dogs on a leash.*

✿ *Protect and do not disturb wildlife.*

✿ *Use the trail at your own risk.*

✿ *Leave only your thanks and footprints - take nothing but photographs.*